Torah

Portions

Journal

ISBN: 978-1-522-70462-1

FamilyBuddy
PO Box 429
Granger IN 46530-0429

ABOUT THIS SCHEDULE

This daily Torah reading schedule was formulated based on the traditional 54-week Torah (Instruction) reading schedule. Daily scheduled readings are divided by the author and are portioned in order to help the reader get through each week's portions by studying smaller portions each day. Read two portions each day for weeks that are combined.

SUGGESTIONS FOR USE

Read the day's Scriptures and reflect on what they mean to your life today. Make a note of questions you think of while reading. Jot down other Scripture that comes to mind.

When you begin a new book, keep this book handy to look back at your insights and questions from your previous study. See how you've grown over the past year. See what questions you are still wondering about.

The author has included a daily Proverb portion schedule based on matching the day of the month with the corresponding chapter. (On the third day of the month, read the third chapter of Proverbs.) Rather than read the whole chapter, there are just a few verses to read each day. You can cut out the pages and use them as a bookmark, if you like.

GENESIS 1:1-2:3

WEEK 1 ● DAY 3
GENESIS 3

GENESIS 5

GENESIS 6:1-8

GENESIS 7

GENESIS 8

Genesis 9

GENESIS 10

GENESIS 12

GENESIS 14

GENESIS 16

GENESIS 17

GENESIS 18:1-15

GENESIS 18:16-33

Genesis 22

GENESIS 23

GENESIS 24:22-51

GENESIS 25:12-18

GENESIS 25:19-34

Genesis 26:1-16

GENESIS 26:17-35

Genesis 27:1-17

GENESIS 27:18-40

GENESIS 28:10-22

GENESIS 29:1-30

GENESIS 30:25-43

GENESIS 31:22-32:2

GENESIS 34

GENESIS 35:1-15

GENESIS 38:1-19

WEEK 9 • DAY 5
GENESIS 39

GENESIS 40

Genesis 41:1-40

GENESIS 44:1-17

GENESIS 46:1-27

GENESIS 46:28-47:12

EXODUS 1

EXODUS 2:1-10

Exodus 3

EXODUS 4

EXODUS 7:8-24

EXODUS 9:8-35

EXODUS 10:1-20

EXODUS 12:43-51

EXODUS 13:17-14:31

EXODUS 16

EXODUS 17:1-7

EXODUS 17:8-16

WEEK 17 ● DAY 1
EXODUS 18:1-12

EXODUS 19:14-25

EXODUS 20:18-26

EXODUS 22:1-15

EXODUS 23:1-19

EXODUS 23:20-33

EXODUS 24

EXODUS 25:31-40

EXODUS 27:1-8

EXODUS 27:9-19

WEEK 20 ● DAY 2
EXODUS 28:6-14

EXODUS 28:31-43

EXODUS 33

EXODUS 35:1-29

EXODUS 37:1-24

EXODUS 37:25-38:7

Week 23 • Day 1

Exodus 38:21-31

Exodus 39:1-7

LEVITICUS 3

Leviticus 4

LEVITICUS 5:1-13

LEVITICUS 8

LEVITICUS 10

Leviticus 11:1-12

Leviticus 13:38-46

LEVITICUS 15:1-12

LEVITICUS 27:14-25

NUMBERS 1

NUMBERS 2

Numbers 3:1-20

NUMBERS 3:40-51

NUMBERS 5:1-10

NUMBERS 6

NUMBERS 7

NUMBERS 10:11-36

NUMBERS 12

NUMBERS 13:1-25

NUMBERS 16:35-50

NUMBERS 18:1-7

NUMBERS 18:8-32

NUMBERS 20:1-13

Numbers 21:1-20

NUMBERS 21:21-35

NUMBERS 22:1-20

NUMBERS 23:1-12

NUMBERS 33:1-49

NUMBERS 35:6-34

NUMBERS 36

DEUTERONOMY 3:1-11

DEUTERONOMY 11:1-25

DEUTERONOMY 20

Week 50 • Day 1

Deuteronomy 26:1-15

DEUTERONOMY 29:9-15

DEUTERONOMY 31:1-8

DEUTERONOMY 31:24-30

DEUTERONOMY 32:1-9

DEUTERONOMY 32:19-27

Deuteronomy 32:28-38

Daily Proverbs

January	February	March	April
1:1-3	1:4-6	1:7	1:8-9
2:1-2	2:3-5	2:6	2:7-8
3:1-2	3:3-4	3:5-8	3:9-10
4:1-2	4:3-4	4:5-6	4:7-9
5:1-4	5:5	5:6	5:7-9
6:1-3	6:4-5	6:6-8	6:9-11
7:1-3	7:4-5	7:6-9	7:10-12
8:1-4	8:5-7	8:8-9	8:10-11
9:1-2	9:3	9:4	9:5-6
10:1-3	10:4-6	10:7-9	10:10-12
11:1-3	11:4-6	11:7-9	11:10-12
12:1-3	12:4-6	12:7-9	12:10-11
13:1-2	13:3-4	13:5-6	13:7-9
14:1-3	14:4-6	14:8-9	14:10-12
15:1-3	15:4-5	15:3-8	15:9-11
16:1-2	16:3-5	16:6-8	16:9-11
17:1-2	17:3-4	17:5-6	17:7-8
18:1-2	18:3-4	18:5-6	18:7-8
19:1-3	19:4-5	19:6-7	19:8-9
20:1-3	20:4-6	20:7-9	20:10-12
21:1-2	21:3-5	21:6-8	21:9-11
22:1-3	22:4-6	22:7-9	22:10-12
23:1-3	23:4-5	23:6-8	23:9-11
24:1-2	24:3-6	24:7-10	24:11-12
25:1-3	25:4-5	25:6-7a	25:7b-10
26:1-3	26:4-6	26:7-9	26:10-11
27:1-2	27:3-5	27:6-7	27:8-9
28:1-3	28:4-6	28:7-9	28:10-11
29:1-2		29:3-5	29:6-7
30:1-4		30:5-6	30:7-10
31:1-7		31:8-9	

DAILY PROVERBS

May	June	July	August
1:10-16	1:17-19	1:20-21	1:22-23
2:9-11	2:12-13	2:14	2:15
3:11-12	3:13-18	3:19-20	3:21-24
4:10-12	4:13-15	4:16	4:17
5:10	5:11-12	5:13-14	5:15-16
6:12-15	6:16-18	6:19	6:20-22
7:13-15 (7-10)	7:16-18 (7-10)	7:19-20 (7-10)	7:21 (7-10)
8:12-14	8:15-18	8:19-21	8:22-26
9:7	9:8	9:9	9:10
10:13-15	10:16-18	10:19-21	10:22-24
11:13-15	11:16-18	11:19-21	11:22-23
12:12-13	12:14-15	12:16-17	12:18-20
13:10-11	13:12 & 15	13:13-14	13:16-17
14:13-15	14:16-18	14:19-21	14:22-24
15:12-14	15:15-17	15:18-20	15:21-23
16:12-14	16:15-16	16:17-19	16:20-22
17:9-10	17:12-13	17:14-15	17:16-18
18:9-10	18:11-12	18:13-14	18:15-16
19:10-11	19:12-14	19:15-17	19:18-19
20:13-15	20:16-18	20:19-20	20:21-22
21:12-13	21:14-16	21:17-19	21:20-22
22:13-14	22:15-16	22:17-19	22:20-21
23:12-14	23:15-18	23:19-21	23:22-23
24:13-14	24:15-18	24:19-22	24:23-25
25:11-12	25:13-14	25:15-17	25:18-20
26:12-13	26:14-15	26:16-17	26:18-19
27:10-11	27:12-13	27:14-16	27:17-18
28:12-13	28:14-15	28:16-17	28:18-20
29:8-10	29:12-13	29:14-16	29:17-18
30:11-14	30:15-16	30:17	30:18-20
31:10-14		31:15-18	31:19-22

DAILY PROVERBS

September	October	November	December
1:24-26a	1:26b-27	1:28-31	1:32-33
2:16-17	2:18-19	2:20	2:21-22
3:25-26	3:27-28	3:29-32	3:33-35
4:18-19	4:20-22	4:23-24	4:25-27
5:17-18	5:19	5:20	5:21-23
6:23-26	6:27-29	6:30-33	6:34-35
7:22-23 (7-10)	7:24-25 (11-23)	7:26 (11-23)	7:27 (11-23)
8:27-30a	8:30b-31	8:32-33	8:34-36
9:11	9:12	9:13-15	9:16-18
10:25-26	10:27-28	10:29-30	10:31-32
11:24-25	11:26-27	11:28-29	11:30-31
12:21-22	12:23-24	12:25-26	12:27-28
13:18-19	13:20-21	13:22-23	13:24-25
14:25-27	14:28-30	14:31-32	14:33-35
15:24-25	15:26-28	15:29-31	15:32-33
16:23-25	16:26-28	16:29-30	16:31-33
17:19-21	17:22-24	17:25-26	17:27-28
18:17-18	18:19-20	18:21-22	18:23-24
19:20-22	19:23-25	19:26-27	19:28-29
20:23-24	20:25-26	20:27-28	20:29-30
21:23-24	21:25-27	21:28-29	21:30-31
22:22-23	22:24-26	22:26-27	22:28-29
23:24-25	23:26-28	23:29-33	23:34-35
24:26-27	24:28-29	24:30-32	24:33-34
25:21-22	25:23-24	25:25-26	25:27-28
26:20-21	26:22-23	26:24-26	26:27-28
27:19-20	27:21-22	27:23-24	27:25-27
28:21-22	28:23-24	28:25-26	28:27-28
29:19-21	29:22-23	29:24-25	29:26-27
30:21-23	30:24-28	30:29-31	30:32-33
	31:23-26		31:27-31

Made in the USA
San Bernardino,
CA